The Lanterns We Carry

Sarah Heist

BookLeaf Publishing

India | USA | UK

Presentation by *BookLeaf Publishing*

Web: www.bookleafpub.com

E-mail: info@bookleafpub.com

ISBN: 9789360949808

First edition 2024

To the infinitely iridescent & incredible people in my life known as Clardys-

Thank you for making this first book of mine possible.

To my readers- may the words within these pages bring you comfort & insight for all the days and phases of your life.

Day 1

It is so very hard
To be a person
Who delights in truth,
Clarity,
Upfront understanding
And empathy.

To be this person
And exist in a world
Of mixed signals
Feigned interest
Miscommunication
And apathy-
It is nigh unto suffocating.

It is so nice
That there are things like
Naps,
purring cats,
soft lights,
And moments where
There is nothing else to
Concern yourself with
Except the next breath-
While beginning to enjoy the feeling of solitude
For the very first time.

Day 2

As sunlight shines through you
Casting rainbows on the floor
Light to all in need of more
Congratulations
A new high score

I welcome you to the new day
Arms wide in ecstatic glee
How lovely it is
That you survived another day
Like me.

Beloved, I see your stained-glass self
I see your mosaic mind.
I see where you took your broken peace
And chose bravely to be kind

To yourself
And everyone else

I know you didn't start this way
I know that it took great pain
I know you wanted life to end that day
I know it feels insane

Your. mosaic. matters.
the process it took for you to get where you
stand
In this iteration of you
A stranger in a new land

Impressive is an understatement
Like trees growing out of pavement

You've come so brilliantly far.
From the first day you learned you were made of
glass
By feeling yourself shattered
Scattered on the grass
From a word hurled like stone

I know you've felt so alone
And maybe even without a home
Or safety net
Better yet,
Even any place to rest.

I see you, mosaic-maker
You with such great heart
I see the reddish brown edges
Where you rebuilt yourself
By yourself
Into this brilliant work of art

Beloved, I wish you to rest
Relax in the moment and just be
Stare in wonder
Be torn asunder
At all you've done
How far you've come

Look in awe
With me

You, out of whatever force you use to bind you,
Armed with will and hope
Made beauty from brokenness
And found new ways to cope

What great lengths you went through
To find you

If this doesnt sound applicable
If you're saying sadly
"That's not me."
Just keep going, love.
I promise you're not despicable

It'll take hard work
And the patience of time
Putting together your pieces
Is to dance on a hair-fine line

Wanted to include this important note:
Healing is INCONVENIENT
I'm sorry but it had to be wrote.

Someday, maybe even now
As you're starting to perceive
If only but through a keyhole stare
You're seeing
Becoming aware
And beginning to believe

Watch
Worry not with how

Witness:
You're becoming unstoppable.
Unbreakable
Unshakable
Free.

Day 3

22:
Searching for a way to flow
A thing to extend my dance
And grow
Beyond the confining bounds of
Skin and bone

A memory appears

Fifth grade:
Learning sign language dance
And with ribbon, prance
To holy music

I wonder...

Go to the store
Yellow is my favorite colour
Need a stick
Leave with my purchase,
Hopeful and anticipant

Get to the car
My partner says
"Try it out now"

"Here? In the parking lot?"
"Yeah, why not"

Unwrap
Unclasp & loop through
Shaky hands
Oh god I hope I remember the steps
Connect to...
Big breath

Unfurl
Color swirls-

A streak of yellow as
I let it fly free
Arcing over my head
A mundane lot outside a shop
Now vibrant instead
Joy and glee radiating from me

All the world becomes
Sparkles and sunshine

My little yellow ribbon
So began a journey
Of healing my wounded inner child
And rediscovering
My beauty within

Day 4

Sometimes
You don't know how bad it's gotten
Until you hear it said aloud

"I have food in my fridge that's been there since
I moved in 7 months ago.. Don't peek."
"I haven't showered in a week"

Even though you can smell the reek

"You look like you don't think you're strong
enough"
"I hope you never hurt anyone else the way that
you hurt me"
"I can't have any part of you in my life"

It would probably be more painless if only they
had used a knife

It is such an interesting thing
To be blindsided by your own reality
To have no concept of how you got here
Until you start to take it apart
Piece by piece

The minutes start to make sense
The hours account to recompense
The actions you did
Or didn't do
What you said
Or didn't say

And all the days you didn't pray
To your God
Asking, pleading
To be shown the way
To peace and softness
How to be still
How to be kind

You can feel all you like
You can want it with all your heart
You can dress it up
Say the lines
Play the part

And yet
With all that
You can hurt at the drop of a hat
Yourself
And everyone else.

Remember:
Don't erase your experience

Or think you're a pretender
With the words
"Not that bad"

Return that shit to sender.

To be considered serious
All you need for it to be is
"Just bad enough."

It's not being delirious-
You can drown in an inch of water.

Day 5

I want
To dance under the waterfall I was born near
To listen to every song I could ever want to hear
To do everything that causes me fear
To sew my own closet with fabrics solid, stretch,
and sheer

I want to travel to Thailand because I crave
curry
I want to visit Japan and enjoy a moment of not
having to hurry
I want to taste all the sweet and bitter and
umami
And I don't want to have to say sorry
For doing what I want

I want to dance in front of a giant crowd
I want to sing so very LOUD
I want fire to spark from my fingers
And to collaborate with my favorite singers

I want to follow my dreams
I want to scream
I want to be every single thing I ever dreamed of
being

I want my younger self to be proud of me
I want my older self to have memories to share
with glee
I want my present self to just be
Happy.

I want to heal
I want my healed self to be my greatest reveal
I want to help
I want to swim like mermaid amongst kelp
I want to adopt and foster children
I want to take destroyed things and help rebuild
them
I want to travel with cats
Wipe my feet on so many mats
I want to write & recite
I want to read and never again bleed
I want to paint without constraint

I want my life on a page and everyone to be
amazed at how far I went with where I started
from
I want to inspire
And perspire
I want to get to the end of my days knowing that
all I achieved
I did for and by myself
Because I believed

And I didn't settle for being a doll on a shelf

And
I want to share all of this with
Someone
Share the fun
Share the tears
Share the laughs
Share the fears
Hold my hand
Walk together through all these strange lands
Live until our knees are sore
And we can't adventure anymore

Then
I want to rest
My head on their chest
Keep holding hands
Until the next life
Until the next new land
Until the last grain of sand
Falls

Day 6

Let your victim die.

Do not carry your hostage
Your broken and mangled
Hair matted and tangled
With blood

There is no point in keeping them alive
There is no possibility for them to survive
And to thrive
Would be a death sentence.
Let alone carrying them around-
Only trouble will -
And does- abound.

You do not have to keep that story
You don't have to relive your trauma
as if it's your glory
There is no pride
in never learning how to let things subside
Or to create unnecessary drama
Because chaos is more comfortable than peace

You self sabotage before a dry-cleaned shirt can
create a crease

Your vindication comes from a confirmation of
your beliefs
Denial and distraction is your relief

Accountability
Stability
Accepting inevitability of consequence due to
action
(Or inaction)
Understanding that you are not owed closure and
satisfaction-
If your unhealed trauma is your toxicity
The ONLY WAY OUT is through
Authenticity.

Know this:
You are worth getting better
You are worth removing your dis-ease
You're allowed to heal
You're allowed to know beauty
You're not damned to cruelty-

It is necessary to feel
All the suck and guck and being shit outta luck
But then you must stop

Let your victim die

Let the story close

Let the chapter end with a full send
Yes it'll be scary
Yes it'll be like changing your identity-
As you discard an entire entity
But remember how bad was the one that you had
How much pain with no gain
The space between the disparity
Of who you want to be
Versus
Who you let yourself seem.

Let. Your victim. Die.

Embrace a new life
It's not like it'll be free of strife.
But it'll be yours
And you'll be free
Finally free
To just be.

Day 7

Do you walk the Wonderland Way?

Do you understand the things that everyone does
say?
Or do you, like me, see only nonsense in the
day-to-day

Have you seen through the keyhole
To the gardens beyond
Listening to flowers' siren song
Have you looked, searched for the rabbit with
the coat
Or tried to swim the moat-
Traversing your own tears and facing your
deepest fears?

Do you know about ravens and writing desks
(And how there's no answer to that)
And have you found the beauty inside a hat
Or a wing of a bat?

For that is the Wonderland Way
It is accepting the nonsense with grace
It's skipping and dancing with lobsters and
knowing you won't leave a trace

All around you is beauty, my child
Even in the weird and the wild
There's visual sugar to taste
Mad creatures to meet and greet
(Or escape with haste)
It's all a-part of this infinite, intricate place.

Follow the Wonderland Way
There are infinite fun games to play
Your mind you won't find
"Who are you?" A question most true
But your soul won't be tolled
If only you begin your practice today

Loosen your grip on what is
Release the control you think you hold
And embrace the madness within
(I promise the pleasure isn't a sin)

I'm not here to guarantee bliss
But to say that you won't be remiss
If you stay awhile
Within moon-shone Cheshire's smile
You might just feel Life's kiss

Follow the Wonderland Way,
My love
Follow with wings soft and light as a dove

You'll be looking below
While standing above
And if you wish it I can help with a shove

Down the rabbit hole.

Day 8

I will become strong enough to be soft
I will forge myself into iron capable of
withstanding vulnerability
I will have boundaries so firmly carved that it
will be a delight for others not to cross them
I will love myself fiercer & with more passion
I will love myself to the end of never wanting to
harm or hold anger towards another being
I will love my dark thoughts that try to distract
me
I will embrace discomfort as though it were a
long-lost old friend
My joy will radiate
My sorrow will too
I will know how to gracefully navigate turmoil-
Like singing in a sandstorm
I will be the master mosaic-maker of my pieces
as I remake and re-break myself as many times
as it take to understand the true meaning of
taking everything lightly

You will look on me with awe and confusion
You will ask me how and why
Why involves suffering
Some I went through

Some others go through
Everywhere, everyday
It exists as long as you're willing to accept the
suffering of suffering
Which leads me to How-
One day you wake up, take a look at your life, &
imagine a new one
Then you do whatever it takes
Whatever It Takes
To create it
Why?
Because I had a choice-
I could die so easily and so early
Or
I could live
If I wanted to live I had to figure out how I was
going to find or make a life worth living

Life is paradox . Existence is chaos.
Glorious, iridescent, & organized chaos
No-thing happens without cause or reason
Everything is written, yet you- at any moment-
Can rewrite your stars
Once you embrace the paradox, you can begin
prioritizing

Who is the most important person in your life?
If asked to make a list of all you love, how long
would it be 'till you named yourself?

Are you truly doing your best?

Acceptance is easy
Mediocrity as a form of death is easy as cake
Succumbing to the numb suffering is a
whispered lullaby in a dream
But the discomfort of feeling-
Of rejecting and questioning all you ever know
for the sake of growing?
Running headfirst towards the shattering of all
you ever found comfort in simply to find out the
meaning of "real" or "reality"?
That.
Is an agonizing bliss.
That is being a Warrior of Love
I am a Warrior of Love
Are You?
Would You?
Will you?

Day 9

In case you were wondering or thought you
could cheat
There is truly no hack-
No system to beat.

There is no half way.

You can't half-skydive
Half-start your own enterprise
you can't half-fall in love
Half-accept your gifts from Above

You can't half decide
To end your life
Or
Stay alive
You don't half fall on your face
You don't half stand back up
And you aren't granted half grace

Jesus didn't half die
Yoda didn't suggest you half try
MLK didn't dream of half equality
(Sidenote: you can't deliver a half apology)
Frida Kahlo didn't half paint

She wasn't known as "Catherine the half Great"
Dorothea Dix didn't half change modern
psychology
And you shouldn't half enjoy any and all
frivolity

Be wholly here
Be wholly yourself
Realize this power is what will bring you true
wealth
Don't ever become complacent with living life
on a shelf
Make complete choices
Dim the other noises
Take accountability
Or credit
Grow in stability
Or edit
The whole of what way
You wish to go

(Psssst- you decide this today)

You are a whole person
Exactly as you exist
With all that makes you who you are
As bright and beautiful as any old star
Please-
Persist.

Don't try for a half life
Don't half chase your dreams
Don't let fear cloud your mind
Remember near-to-nothing is as it seems

Even the moon in its phases is still one whole
Great & wonderful
Celestial being
And it does not apologize for turning tides
Or intense feeling.

Day 10

My love I wrote to you once
The words lost like sand sieved and scattered
through a shattered hourglass
Your favorite tool of time

So let me write to you again

Let me tell you of how I've dreamed you would
come
Prayed for your kiss
Fantasized about your sweet release at a single
brush of your fingertips

I love to watch you work
And I know you've been busy lately
It never gets old to see how gently you escort
these souls
Away from their bodies
As soft and gentle
As a last exhale

But my love I must confess
In this letter I must write anew
For while I do still ache and crave
The bliss of your inevitable,

Final kiss

I have been seeing someone else.
I have tasted sunlight on my tongue
Felt warmth flood my cheeks
I have danced in their grasp
Have breathed in their scent

Yes, my love,
Life has held my hand.

And while it is a wild ride
And there are many times I wish for your rest
And to lay forever in peace by your side-

I know that I would get restless again
And wish for something new
So without leaving early
And making preemptive strike
I think I'll keep my date with Life
And go on a little hike

I'll feel laughter in my chest
The rumble of sound vibrating molecules
miraculously
(Does Life's wonder not end?)
I'll sing with great vibrato
And cry to sate intensity
I'll eat and feel full

Fall in love and feel pain
And joy
And loss
And relief
And heartache
And pleasure
And grief

And oh my love
I can't wait to explain
About all my adventures
And with no shame
At the end of it all
I'll keep our date
I'll lie with you and wait
For the next time when
I can play Life's game

Please, my love,
Don't hurry
Don't wait outside my door
I've decided I'm not done yet
With wading on Life's shore
I'm sorry I'm such a fickle lover-

One day pleading, begging for you
The next I'm praying I don't see your face or feel
your embrace
Until I'm quite old and sore

Please
Do believe me
As I've said before
I do long for your rest
And waiting for it feels like a test,
Some days even a chore.

But, my dear Death,
I do think I'll wait just a little more.

Day 11

I am an Ancient Child
A paradox, a concept,
Most often a conundrum

I am the flower that grows through the cement
I am the ray of sunshine that peeks through the
clouds
I am the candlelight in the darkness
That you can't snuff out

I am also the first tear that falls
When your heart is much too heavy
I am the straw on the camels back
And the weight that breaks the levy

I am comfort and courage
Pain and disdain
I am made of all the growth I've gotten
Through all my understanding

I see you in your darkness
I celebrate your Light
I can help you through your deepest fears
I can hold you so very tight

I will also challenge you
Challenge with how I change
I am fantastic chameleon
With an impossibly wide range
More than that-
I mentioned growth.
Of which I do everyday
That is the only goal, you see
Though it may come off as strange.

I am an Ancient Child
And I am not alone
To find another like me
Just look for those with a dash of whimsy
Those with wisdom in their eyes
Go ask a twirling pixie
On how they see through a disguise
Ask further still their thoughts on life
And everything in between
(Especially fun is all the unseen)

Give them love
Tell them to rest
For God's sake, feed their hungry
(Mind, body, & soul)
Let them in to your world
Don't worry about the toll
It'll be a wild ride for sure-
But one of the very best.

Day 12

I grew up in a divided home
Her way was right
His way was wrong
Creating a divide
Two separate sides
Of me
And people wonder
Why I struggle to get along
With myself
Or anyone else

Day 13

I am a magician
In real time
No lie
I can transform anyone
Person, girl, or guy
Into whatever they like
With a wave of my brush
And a flourish of fabric
I can craft the cleverest disguise

Do ye wish to be cat?
With eyes bright green and stripes of blue and
black?
Or dragon with opalescent scales and chainmail
and red tinged scar over one eye?
Or maybe one of the raging undead
And I'll ask you to tell me how you died
instead...

The possibilities are endless
Infinite as imagination itself

There is more magick in shapeshifting than one
would suppose
It goes beyond a nice photo with a cool pose

There's a moment of breath
A space to take away
In becoming something else
Unusual from the everyday

"If I can look in the mirror and see not myself
For a little while
I won't have to deal with the problems I face"
The fears that take chase
The ceaseless chatter
The awful clatter
The noises and the voices and the consequences
of all my choices...
All disappear
And I can see clear
For a moment

And the accolades are nice
The smiles are bright
Laughing at the ones who can't help but look
twice
To see the look on kids' faces once they see what
magic my brush has done
Is more beautiful to me
Than any plain face I could see
I struggle to think of anything more fun

So a magician I have become
Granting any and all a moment

To see a different them
Or a truer one
To see in a mirror
Maybe a bit clearer
Giving them a chance to realize

"Hey maybe...
I can be in control of my life."

Day 14

There is no scent more offensive to me than
asphalt
The acrid stench that promises only death to the
ground below
No sight I hate more to see than destruction-
deforestation of any kind
People or trees

So many scream save the planet
Do everything you can
The planet doesn't need saving
We only destroy ourselves
By our own hands.

My favorite image in any movie
My favorite scene on any screen
Is when there's green and lush overgrowth
Taking control of cities

Cars with trees growing through them
Skyscrapers covered in vines
I root and cheer for all the plants here
And relish the thought when we're gone
When birds can sing their true song

And nature has it's time to sigh with breath soft
and severe
Finally alone with all who revere
Appreciating the moment
When Nature gets to be in their prime
And the planet will belong
To those who truly own it.

Day 15

Sapiosexual
It's contextual
You want to access my body?
First you must glide through my mind.
Are you brave enough to handle what you might
find?

Treat me like your favorite book
(If you don't have one, don't even bother to look)
Slide your fingers lovingly down my well-worn
spine
Know you're still 20,000 leagues from being
able to call me "mine"
Highlight and recite your favorite phrases
Flipping through my pages
Eager to know more
Not skipping to the end in a rush
But taking it all in
As if in a holy hush
Kiss my cover not for its beauty
But for all that lies within
Welcome to chapter 1, my Love.
Let's begin.

Day 16

Words that make up me
Based on what others have seen:

adaptable, adept, adroit, animalistic, apathetic,
Artist, artistic, Ashalerian, augerer, autodidact,
awakened, bacchanalious, beautiful,
Breathtaking, Candy, capricious, caring,
Celestial, chameleonic, Childlike, chimeral,
clock, Cloud, Colorful, cosmic, creative,
demiurgic, dream, dreamer, effervescent,
electrifying, Elegant, Enchanting, Energetic,
Enigmatic, Ephemeral, ethereal, ever-evolving,
Expression, Fae, fated, fetching, fiery, Feisty,
Forest, Free, friend, Fun, Gentle, giggle,
glowing, Goddess, gracious, heart, Honest,
illusory, indefatigable, indifferent, indignant,
indiscreet, ineffable, inevitable, ingenious,
innocence, insatiable, Inspiring, Intriguing,
Jellyfish, knavish, Love, love, loving, loyal,
magical, masochistic, Matrixian, Mercurial,
Moon, multitiered, Nymph, obdurate, obtuse,
paint, passionate, peaceful, Perfect, permanent,
Persephone, perspicacious, philosophical,
playful, precocious, primal, Prism, procurable,
prophetic, pythian, Quiet, quixotic, radiating,

rainbow, Raw, romantic, rough, Seeking,
self-actualized, self-aware, selfish, Sensual,
serendipitous, serene, Shapeshifter, Silhouette,
sly, smile, Smooth, soft, soft spoken,
Spellbinding, spirit, Stunning, talented,
tenacious, tender, thinks outside the box, Gentle,
thoughtful, tough, unapologetic, uncouth,
unique, vibrant, whimsical, wonderland

Day 17

I don't struggle to survive-
I've done that all my life.
The things that get me
The pitfalls that beset me
Is the everyday
The small moments
The mundane
Remembering to put the trash out
Sweep the floor
Eat
Repeat

I can handle the extraordinary
Skipping at 10 feet tall
Prancing as a faerie
Completely transforming
The normal and boring
To something fantastic-
Wonderful and soaring
I can do that in my sleep
I don't give a bleep.

But to maintain consistency?
Go farther than the distance seen
Creating a steady daily routine?

It escapes me.
Infuriates me.
I get angry at my body for needing rest
Needing resets
And when I don't take them
I break then
I've needed a cane
More than once.
I've visited the world of insanity
And felt like a complete dunce
Because i struggle so damn hard to maintain
mundanity
The paradox is enough to make me spew
profanity
Profusely.
Fuck, I confuse me.

Inhale
Exhale
Reset-

Enough water drops can shatter a mountain
Here's to hoping my will can be an infinite
fountain
And one day
The shattering of rocks
Will be unlocking this damn puzzle box
Of my brain.

Day 18

There is so little thought to the role of a
seamstress
Threading a needle
Putting together a dress
But it is and always has been so much more
Let me settle the score

To sew is to See
The threads that bind together Everything
To see with hawk-eye view
Exactly where to cut and glue
When to pin and what to drape
Knowing everything one must do
To leave one's mouth agape
With methods unique and tried-and-true
Forming patterns within paradoxes
(Some going mad for what's inside hat boxes)

It is of the most ancient and sacred of skills
Going far, far beyond any sequins and satin and
frills
From the biblical Adam and Eve
The very first cloth was sewn
Covering the nakedness of the first bodies to
leave the Garden alone

To sew is to See
The fabric that makes up the cosmos
To have your thimble-covered fingertip on
almost
Grasping the spindle and loom that weaves all
that was and all that is to be
Whether joyous or full of doom
Trusting in yourself and your skill every step of
the way
Accepting that you'll learn a new thing almost
every single day

It is referenced in every culture
So many movies, books, & songs
Some I'm sure you've sang along
The Lady of Shalot
The Red Thread of Fate
String Theory
Quantum Entanglement
Concepts that stretch your minds
Now discussing the elasticity that binds...

Blessed are those who sew
Blessed are they made of the calm kindness and
patience it takes
To handle the fabrics of torn hearts and
crestfallen fates
And with careful precision,

Clear-sighted Vision
Mend and patch and create
A new pathway of thought
A new fiber-formed gate

Now every time you put on your clothes
Think with deep gratitude
For the ones who sew
Those who weave the cloth
Form the thread
Bind it all together
So that you can wear and shed
Whatever you wish
However you express
Be it pants, shirt, shoes, or dress

And if you are of the lucky few who know
A person that does sew
Or better yet
If you are such a one
Never forget
How sacred and special
Is a seamstress.

Day 19

"The simple act of trying to love yourself shows
that you do love yourself."

Sarah, I Love You
And the deeper I learn how to Love, the better I
get at showing you
I Love You
One day you'll feel it too
Know it's true
I. Love. You.

You are so incredible.
You've been through so much.
You've experienced almost every kind of touch
You've suffered pain and sickness and sorrow
and grief
Joy and laughter and wonder and relief
Through everything
Everything
You still choose to be-
Kind
And with sound mind
You're so deeply, innately, determined to grow
Like flowers growing through concrete-
What a show.

I Love You-
It exists in every swipe of ChapStick on your
lips
Every bite of food
Every dish that's cleaned
Every song that's sing-ed
Every bit of growth
Every time we don't choke
On speaking the words that express what we're
feeling
On continuing to breathe even when we're
reeling

I Love You
I've been saying it since the last time I cut into
our skin
Since the last time I let our intrusive thoughts
win
Since the last drink I had
Since the last time I let myself be hurt by a man
who didn't see
Or care to appreciate
the precious gift that is me.

My love is still imperfect
(Ha, you are my love- that joke was worth it)
And I'm still learning
In spite of my shadow parts

How to make loving me
My new favorite form of arts

I Love You
And it's been difficult to understand how
everyone sees
This beautiful, capable, talented, skilled,
iridescent creature of light that I am
Except me.

My vision is getting fixed
I'm trying new glasses on for size
And I think between these words and my actions
A new sense of appreciation
And passion for Me
Will be my prize

I Love You, Sarah
Now & until the end of time.

Day 20

My Inky binky boo
Oh how I love you
The feistiest Heist
That never thinks twice
You Rorschach test of a cute kitty fool
It's been a decade that I've had you
Ten whole years since mom found you
Tiny little flea covered mess
Runt of the litter
Feral mom no less
She saved your life then
You've saved mine since
The only thing alive
That's witness my entire journey hence
From simply survival to full revival
You skitchy sketchy thing
Oh how I adore your entire being
With your multicolored paws
And your non-retractable claws
But when your purrs resound
And your tail curls around
Mmmmm... It makes my heart sing.

Thank you for being with me.

Day 21

Persephone
Goddess of Spring
Queen of the Dead
Made of flowers and laughter
Wrath and what comes after
Sovereign in mind of all beings
Who chose to have Hades beside her in bed
Blessed is she who CHOSE to dwell in the dark
Who dove into her shadows
Who retrieved the Sacred Spark

Beloved is she who carries with worthy might
A soft, yet steady,
Lantern's Light.

Like Alice who followed rabbit down hole
She journeyed to the dark and the strange
Becoming a mage with fortified soul

She returns every spring
Goes down every fall
Bringing her Lantern
Throughout it all
It is not with force
Nor with any judgment, malice, or ill-will

But a simple, glass-protected flame
Kindness as it's name-
Holding it patient, sure, and still.

Remember dear child, if nothing else-
That you carry a Lantern Light with your own
will.
You hold her might
Her strength
Her hope
And through the darkest nights
The worst sights
And deepest seas made from all your heaving,
heavy crying
You too can stay afloat
And maybe one day-
You'll catch yourself flying.

May this reminder join these now written
chorusing songs
Adding to The Lanterns We Carry

ACKNOWLEDGEMENT

The amount of people I have to thank is as long of a list as those I have ever met in this short time I've spent on our little blue marble, however there are ones who I would be remiss in not mentioning here.

To my mother- Thank you for raising me, believing in me, and inciting the passion I hold today for the written word.

To everyone else, whether in happiness, healing, or hurt- Thank you for your time, your lessons, and your existence. I wish the best for every single one of you and hope that I have added as much color and depth to your own story as you have to mine.